CUSTOMERS NOW

CUSTOMERS NOW

Profiting From the New Frontier of Content-Based Internet Advertising

How to master two simple content advertising programs—
Google's AdWords content ad network and ContextWeb's
ADSDAQ Exchange—so you can efficiently get your message
out and bring your customers in.

David Szetela

iUniverse, Inc.
New York   Bloomington

Customers Now
Profiting From the New Frontier of Content-Based Internet Advertising

iUniverse books may be ordered through booksellers or by contacting:

iUniverse
1663 Liberty Drive
Bloomington, IN 47403
www.iuniverse.com
1-800-Authors (1-800-288-4677)

Because of the dynamic nature of the Internet, any Web addresses or links contained in this book may have changed since publication and may no longer be valid. The views expressed in this work are solely those of the author and do not necessarily reflect the views of the publisher, and the publisher hereby disclaims any responsibility for them.

ISBN: 978-1-4401-7099-7 (pbk)
ISBN: 978-1-4401-7101-7 (cloth)
ISBN: 978-1-4401-7100-0 (ebook)

Library of Congress Control Number: 2009909985

Printed in the United States of America

iUniverse rev. date: 10/30/09

To my exceptionally wonderful, talented family
– my kids, Michael, Franny, and Aimee, and my wife Wils.

I am awed by you and more grateful than I could ever express
for the love, company and laughter-filled adventures we share.

Praise for Customers Now: Profiting From the New Frontier of Content Based Internet Advertising

"It's about time Search Engine Marketers realized that "Content" is not "Search." Smart advertisers get that fact and make full use of Content Networks to increase their ROI, but if you are one of those who keeps trying to run your content campaigns like your search campaigns, stop right now and read this book. It will open your eyes to all the possibilities that the Content Networks offer."
- Mary O'Brien, Chairman, PPC Summits

"A fundamentally sound and very current look at the opportunities in content network advertising. I recommend that my competition NOT read this book."
– Jeff Hudson, ThePPCBook.com

"Search marketing in the content-driven world is very different from search marketing in the keyword-driven, and I can't think of anyone who understands those differences better than David Szetela. Every search marketer should read this book and follow its advice closely. It might hurt a little to learn all these things – both dramatic and subtle – that nobody every told you before, but trust me that sting will subside and the resulting growth and performance improvements will linger for years."
- Craig Danuloff, President, ClickEquations & Author of High Resolution PPC

David gives it ALL up on making serious money via Contextual Advertising! Ground-breaking, valuable work.
- Richard Stokes, President, AdGooroo

Millions of advertising dollars have disappeared down the black hole of Content Advertising. This book finally illuminates the best practices that can turn those losses into profit. Bravo!
- Erik Qualmann, Global Vice President of Online Marketing for EF Education

Even expert PPC advertisers will be surprised to learn that the ground rules for Content Advertising are so different – and simple.
- Addie Conner, Director of Search Marketing, CourseAdvisor

Szetela has taken a microscope to the mechanisms behind contextual advertising – and explains how to profit from the search engines' matching algorithms in a clear, concise way.
- Michael Flores, Media Director, Ardis Health

The advice for designing and testing display ads is priceless all on its own. This book will have advertisers flocking to contextual advertising! - Pat East, President and CEO, Hanapin Marketing

"David is a master Internet marketer who is willing to put his money where mouth is with a performance-based business model. All of his advice is real-world tested and effective. Pick up this book before your competitors do!"
– Tim Ash, CEO of SiteTuners.com and author of *Landing Page Optimization*

CONTENTS

First, many thanks to my friends at ContextWeb, especially Jay Sears, Biff Burns, Derek Brinkman and Ken Lauher, who approached me to write this book, and good-naturedly suffered the inconvenience of my disregard for deadlines. I have appreciated the opportunity to work with all of you, and hope the book fulfills all of your corporate and individual expectations for it.

Thanks also to the sponsors who enable my other writing and speaking engagements – Search Engine Watch, Search Engine Land, Third Door Media, Incisive Media, and especially the wacky pros at Webmasterradio.fm.

I'm especially grateful to the tight community of PPC experts who read manuscripts of this book, unselfishly providing their time and insightful advice – most notably Matt Van Wagner and Marc Poirier, and also Mary O'Brien, Craig Danuloff and Jeff Hudson. It's one of the deepest pleasures of my life to have the privilege to call such brilliant folks my friends.

I save my final and biggest Thank You for my readers and listeners. I'm very appreciative that you find my work worthwhile and useful, and keep coming back for more. I especially enjoy hearing from you for any reason, by email at <u>david@clixmarketing.com</u> and on Twitter where I'm @Szetela.

David Szetela

David@ClixMarketing.com

www.ClixMarketing.com

P.S. For additional information, updates and more, visit www.CustomersNowBook.com.

INTRODUCTION

By reading "*Customers Now: Profiting From the New Frontier of Content-Based Internet Advertising*," you will become fluent in the new language of two of the leading content advertising programs: Google's underutilized Content Network and ContextWeb's ADSDAQ Exchange.

Read this book if:

1. You are "maxed out" on keyword-driven search engine marketing.
2. Your advertising generates fewer leads for new customers and diminishing engagement metrics for existing customers.
3. Your internet marketing needs new ideas and new energy regardless of your company's revenue size, database, or expertise.

What is Content Advertising?

Ten years ago many companies started to become aware of the new possibilities inherent in pay-per-click (PPC) advertising. It became one of the most cost-effective methods of reaching new customers for all companies. Not only are the megabrands using PPC, it is estimated that close to one million small and medium-sized businesses use paid search advertising. It is easy to access, easy to fund and easy to calculate return on investment.

Less well-known is PPC content advertising - a much more pervasive and readily-available advertising opportunity. After reading *Customers Now: Profiting From the New Frontier of Content-Based Internet Advertising* you will become fluent in the new language of two of the leading content advertising programs: Google's underutilized Content Network and ContextWeb's ADSDAQ Exchange. Both programs are easy and inexpensive to use. You can get started on either one of these services for as little as $25 and in as little as twenty-five minutes.

Speed and affordability aside, content-based advertising leads customers down the path of prospect to conversion. Customers today have choices. A lot of them. So before you fulfill the sale, you must generate demand for your product or service. Content-based advertising exposes specific groups of customers to specific products and services better than keyword search can. It gives you access to a giant untapped pool of customers. If you think of the sales process as a funnel, content advertising delivers customers at the top as shown in this example.

Keyword search is about demand fulfillment. For example, a customer that enters "North Face ski jacket" most likely has made up his mind about the purchase. But content advertising is about creating demand. It fuels the funnel by making potential customers aware of North Face ski jackets while looking at web site content about skiing or travel or a destination city. There's a big difference.

As people surf the web, they are exploring information about their interests, while discovering new things that interest them. Grabbing their attention during this research and discovery phase is how you effectively build new demand for your product or service. You are building interest among users that may not even know about your product or your product category.

Content Sites' Advertising Raises Awareness and Message Association Among the Affluent

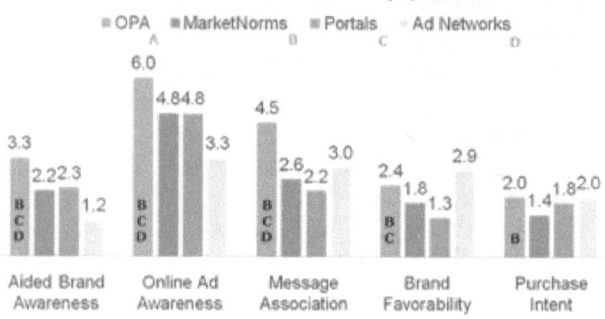

Ad Effectiveness Deltas, $75K+

Source: Dynamic Logic's MarketNorms campaigns over last 3 years through Q1 2009
A/B/C/D indicate statistically significant difference between deltas at .90 CL
OPA N=653; MN=1,458; Portals=451; Ad Networks=87

If you're interested in creating demand for your products and services, this double-pronged search/content attack can reinvigorate your internet marketing strategy. In this book, I'll show you strategies for using content-based services like Google AdWords (AdWords.google.com) and ContextWeb's ADSDAQ Exchange (exchange.contextweb.com), and even give you specific tactics for getting the best results from each of them. Now is the time to educate yourself on effective internet marketing and your company's connection with customers – now.

Chapter 1

The Future Is Content

Legendary adman Jay Chiat once described a round of golf as "very fascinating, very addictive, and incredibly challenging. You're never satisfied. It's kind of like advertising." Chiat didn't live to see the advent of search engine marketing, but his observations fit with what search engine marketing is today. Search engine marketing has come close to satisfying its users with its ability to be measured, analyzed, and optimized. The growth of SEM certainly shows a continued attraction, as advertisers continuously search for that magic keyword that will drive clicks and revenues.

There is still much more ahead for internet marketers. Even if you're a Google AdWords pay-per-click advertiser, one who's getting spectacular results, there's another level. It's very likely that you can increase your profitable sales significantly - by up to 75-100 percent - while at the same time, create more customer demand for your products or services. This not-so-well kept secret comes in the form of learning to mount successful campaigns using a little-understood capability built into Google AdWords, which is advertising on the Google Content Network. It also comes in the form of a new ad exchange that's making it easier for advertisers to mount and manage campaigns: ContextWeb's ADSDAQ Exchange.

AdWords is hardly a secret. Campaigns display ads on search results pages, at the top and right side of the page, when a search is performed on Google and on Google search engine partners (like AOL) - collectively known as the Search Network. The ads displayed are relevant to the person who typed in the search term. Such as this example below, using the term "red sneakers."

Less well-understood is the fact that, by default, ads also appear on web site pages - sites that have chosen to participate in Google's AdSense program to "monetize" their content. When a site visitor clicks on an AdSense ad, the advertiser pays for the click, and Google shares some of the click revenue with the site owner. Google calls this network of sites its Content Network. Here's one example of what an AdSense ad looks like:

Ads by Google
_____

Coffee Exposed
A shocking secret coffee co's don't want you to know
www.coffeefool.com

Advertising on content networks allows advertisers to reach a huge proportion of internet users - many times the number of people who use search services to find specific sites covering specific topics. Even better, advertisers can reach potential customers before they're likely to conduct searches - avoiding crowded ad competition on the search pages. But tapping into this huge network requires specific best practices and techniques that aren't widely known. This book will expose them. Those techniques are often counter-intuitive to PPC advertisers who are accustomed to think in terms of ads displayed as the result of search engine searches, and the best measure of success.

Many AdWords advertisers have tried advertising on Google's AdWords Content Network, only to watch click costs soar while revenues and profits failed to keep pace. Others have shied away from advertising on the Content Network because they've heard that it delivers "poor-quality traffic." But that thinking needs to be re-examined. The truth is that Content Network advertisers can get excellent results: better-than-acceptable conversions (sales or leads) that deliver profitable revenue to the bottom line. The key lies in understanding how Content Networks operate, and adopting best practices in controlling ad placement to attract potential high-quality site visitors (perspective customers).

As mentioned, content-based campaigns display ads on the web pages of site owners who participate in a search engine's ad serving program. Google has AdSense, while Yahoo has Yahoo Publisher Network. Microsoft will soon roll out a similar program. We will spend a fair amount of time in this book detailing the strategies and tactics for successfully using ContextWeb's content based ADSDAQ Exchange.

First let's take a look behind the scenes. How does Google "decide" which ads should be served? Google's ad-matching software examines the words (content) on the web site's pages, and then examines its ad inventory -- PPC ads and associated keywords -- and displays ads that best match the content of the site pages. ADSDAQ's matching software works differently. It matches advertiser-specified Categories with pages within its content network, freeing the advertiser from trying to intuitively decide on keywords that describe such pages. The advertiser gets matched with site visitors who are interested in the relevant ads. The potential customer sees ads that relate to the interests that drew them to the site in the first place. Site owners earn revenue that supports their ability to continue to publish valuable content.

Then why the perception problem with content-based advertising performance? The first is the "last click attribution" obsession. Advertisers place undue importance on the last click before purchase and that obsession often unfairly credits search engine keywords. Compare it to driving down a busy highway filled with billboards. A billboard for a steak restaurant at the beginning of the trip may start the attraction toward the restaurant. A billboard in the middle may push a customer to want to learn more about its menu. Another one may close the deal in the customer's mind. The last one may rate a call for a reservation. All the ads are valuable, but the last one gets the credit.

In the best cases, advertisers have traditionally had to settle for the fact ad response rates - click-through-rates (CTRs), or the ratio of clicks to impressions - have usually been much lower than those they get from search advertising. Even worse, conversion rates for content advertising, the percentage of content-ad-generated site visitors who buy or submit a lead form, are traditionally lower. There are three main reasons for this difference.

First, since content ads are ancillary to web site content, the ads are not actively read as frequently as search ads. At worst, they're considered to be annoying distractions. Second, the software that matches Google keyword/ad group combinations to web site page content is difficult to control -- meaning it sometimes does a poor job of putting together ads with related content. Third, by default, search and content campaigns are "lumped together" in the Web interface advertisers use to control and manage ad campaigns. Advertisers must take extra steps to separate the two. So the default campaign settings force advertisers to use a common interface to manage and report on the two very different campaign types, making it difficult to see and control what's working and what's not. The net result: Many companies pour money into advertising that, in aggregate, results in relatively poor results – especially in terms of ROI. Some advertisers even conclude PPC simply can't work for them, never realizing that search advertising may work well for them, but their content advertising is bleeding so much money in click charges that they deem the whole effort is unprofitable. That's why content campaigns should be run separately from search campaign. And the truth is that if it is properly understood and managed, content advertising can deliver excellent results. It can be close or equal to the CTRs and conversion rates obtainable via search advertising.

There's another under-appreciated but significantly positive effect of advertising on content networks. Even though a smaller proportion of content network impressions and clicks may turn into sales, those impressions helps introduce and reinforce the advertiser's brand. In effect content network advertising can increase the number of people who click on search ads, since they're familiar with the brand name via content ads. Site visitors that arrive via clicking on a content ad may not convert on the first visit, but some come back to the site later and convert.

Smart marketers who employ multiple off-line and online advertising tactics know that the whole effort should be viewed as a "portfolio approach." In other words, no single tactic should be viewed in isolation of the others. For example, an email campaign results in a visitor to a site who doesn't convert on the first visit -- but converts later after viewing a content ad that reinforce the positive impression of the original visit.

Unfortunately, few tools exist for detecting this effect and, at least as importantly, apportioning a value to the pre-conversion actions. It's not tracked and reported by almost all of the web site analytics packages and conversion-tracking software, including the tracking mechanisms used by Google, Yahoo and Microsoft in their PPC systems. It's one of the secrets of search engine marketing, which we'll explore further in the next chapter.

Chapter 2

The Secrets of Content

Content-based advertising is the future of internet advertising as evidenced by Google's data, which shows advertisers continue to spend on search and contextual advertising and untargeted vendors are seeing a downward trend. Google claims its content network consists of several hundred thousand sites, whose aggregate site visitors comprise nearly 75 percent of all internet users in the U.S. The proportion is even higher outside the U.S. For example Google claims that its content network in Germany reaches 89% of all German internet users. The ADSDAQ Exchange launched in 2005. As of May 2008, the ADSDAQ Exchange ranked among the top 20 ad supported properties, according to comScore Media Metrix, and reached more than 115 million monthly unique visitors each month. To give you some idea of how big that number is, consider that Google (with YouTube and Blogger.com) counted 149 million unique visitors in December 2008, according to comScore. The ADSDAQ

Exchange serves impressions from more than 400 advertisers, including 9 out of the top 10 marketing organizations, and more than 9,000 publishers.

The infrastructure is also clearly laid out by each company. According to Google's site *"the technology that drives AdWords contextual advertising comes from Google's award-winning search and page ranking technology. Google continually scans the millions of pages from the content network to look for relevant matches with your keywords and other campaign data. When we find a match, your ad becomes eligible to run on that page. Google's extensive web search and linguistic processing technology can decipher the meaning of virtually any content network page to ensure we're showing the most relevant ads. Then, we match ads that are precisely targeted to the content page based on the associated keywords. For example, if someone visits a web page on astronomy he/she would be served Google AdWords ads for telescopes. Contextual Advertising benefits Web users by linking content with relevant products and services. This is great for Google advertisers like you, because you can now reach more prospective customers on more places on the Web."*

Sounds great, right? You supply the keywords, and Google places your ads on just the pages where your target audience "hangs out," waiting and eager to visit your web site. But in reality, targeting ads to the right site pages requires techniques and best practices that aren't intuitively obvious to advertisers used to targeting ads to search results pages. Fortunately for you, this book details the methods for controlling the content-matching algorithms to laser-target the placement of your ads.

Google links content to products and services. ADSDAQ advertisers target their ads by choosing categories of web pages where they want ads to appear. It has developed and implemented "next generation" algorithms that result in connections between content, advertising and users (potential customers). The system assigns a definition to each web page in the exchange in real time. Then, it matches that definition to a category selected by an advertiser.

For both advertisers and publishers, it's essential to make the most accurate match. It uses ad page context to identify the most accurate category and derive the most relevant match between web page and advertiser. With content, it is not about a single keyword, it's about the category of all the keywords on a targeted web page. Let's illustrate this with the following example, viewed from both sides of the content-based advertising approach. A new resort in St. Lucia has an international budget that needs to stretch across North America, the EU, and Asia. It decides to spend the bulk of the budget on Internet advertising. If it buys the keywords, "St. Lucia," "Caribbean vacation," and "tropical resorts" its ad and link to its website will come up only if those keywords are entered. And the only reason they would be entered is if a potential customer is gathering information for a trip. That customer has already traveled a long way down the sales funnel.

If the St. Lucia resort uses the ADSDAQ approach it will start by choosing the categories it wants to appear in, not the keywords. If it decides it can generate the highest volume of valuable customers from travel content pages, that category is easy to find and the proper ad pages will be selected. The resort can then show ads on all travel pages including business sites that have travel pages, and even investment advice sites that list time shares at resorts. The category approach, connecting to relevant ad pages, can catch customers earlier in the sales funnel.

With this approach, the system can learn to categorize automatically with no human management. The algorithms open up billions of pages of ad inventory in highly targeted, niche categories. This guarantees that ads will appear in appropriate context and on brand-safe content that supports the brand message. As seen in the chart below, valuable customers will share information about key issues, products and services, and they are influenced by many sources of information as well as many categories of information. Content sources are expanding exponentially. For performance advertisers, getting their offers in front of the right audience allows them to meet their performance metrics. Among those performance metrics: Creating customer demand and acquisition.

The frequency of sharing differs not only by source, but by category

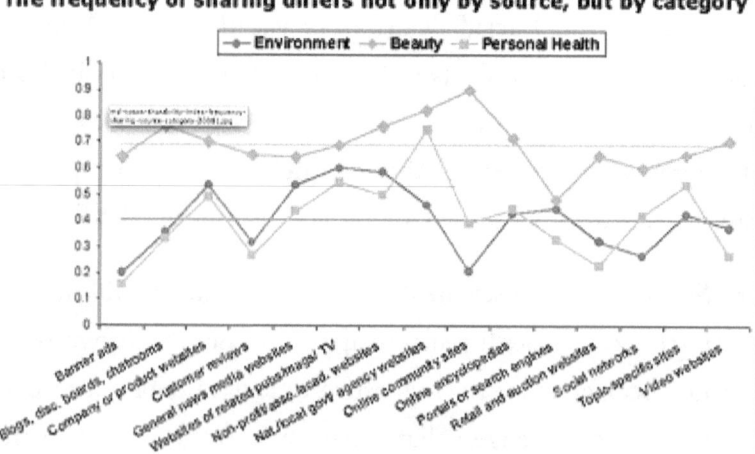

Chapter 3

Something Old; Something New: Merging Keywords and Content

Call it the Britney Spears issue. Especially when she was synonymous with ambulances, psych wards and bad judgment, it seemed like any search phrase a consumer typed in would bring up a Britney Spears gossip story somewhere on the page. If a company sold broccoli spears, and used the word "spears" in its content keyword list, the company's ads could appear on sites with content that described Britney Spears ringtones, or worse. A lot worse.

Keywords will not go away in the new content frontier. But the keywords advertisers use in content ad groups will play a different role than they do for search ads. This is often a tough point for search advertisers to grasp. In search ad groups, keywords are intended to match search queries that are usually related to the advertiser's products and services. Hence, spears will be interpreted as a literal product and never distinguished from a pop star or even long sharp stick. By contrast, the keywords in a content ad group should **describe the types of pages and sites where you want your ads to appear.** So the keyword list for an advertiser's content campaigns should be very different than the keyword lists for search campaigns. Example: A company that sells digital cameras, would use "digital cameras" for a traditional search campaign. It would use, "new mothers, scrapbook sites, parenting advice," and "storing digital photos."

This illustrates one of the main reasons content campaigns garner comparatively low CTRs. Many ads are displayed on irrelevant sites that get heavy traffic. Ad impressions go sky-high while the number of clicks is proportionately very low. But the clicks generated represent new customers, not just buyers at the end of the sales funnel.

Four Best Practices For Creating Content Keyword Lists

1. Always run content campaigns separately from your search campaigns -- i.e., don't simply run one campaign that displays ads on the search and content networks, even though that's the default option when you set up a new campaign. Search engines allow separate content bids in such hybrid campaigns -- don't do it. Create separate search and content campaigns instead.
2. Separate content campaigns into small ad groups -- each with, ideally, 5-15 keywords -- never more than 50.
3. Don't use different match types, such as Google's phrase and exact match. Match type is ignored by the content matching algorithms.

4. Don't separate bid prices for each keyword -- these too are ignored, and Google operates based on the ad group's default bid.

Creating separate search and content campaigns takes a little extra work. To create a separate content campaign, you'll need to edit the campaign's settings just after creating it. Simply uncheck the Google search check box, and check the content network one. Likewise, to create a separate search campaign, un-check the box that directs Google to display ads on its content network.

Most advertisers build keyword lists by relying mainly on intuition more than anything else. An alternative method is more scientific and should provide even more control over where ads appear. Let's start with this assumption: if a keyword-targeted ad group's keywords should describe the pages/sites where an ad should appear, *then possibly the best keyword list is composed of words/phrases that appear most frequently on the target sites' pages.*

A tool is necessary for deriving such lists. Ideally the tool would accept a list of URLs, load every word of content from all pages at the root and in subfolders of that URL, and return a ranked list of one- and two-word keywords. The tool that comes closest is the cryptically named **Textanz** (www.cro-code.com). A bargain at $22.95, this Windows application takes as input any local text file (which can include any web page file), and displays lists of the most frequently-occurring words, as well as lists of frequently-occurring phrases containing any number of words you designate.

Assume for this demonstration that we're building content ad groups for MuscleBound.com, a company that sells bodybuilding equipment. Since the company has a savvy marketing department, they understand their customer demographics very well, and through careful surveys have concluded that there's a high interest in bodybuilding among people who enjoy role-playing games (RPGs).

So MuscleBound has decided that they want their ads displayed on sites frequented by people actively engaged in body-building, and sites frequented by people interested in RPGs. So they need to create two separate keyword-targeted content ad groups.

I used a simple set of tools: the Google AdWords Placement Tool, a simple Google search, and Textanz. Here are the steps to create the keyword lists:

1. Use the AdWords Placement Tool to find ten or so sites within the target categories. The list of possible categories includes one specifically related to bodybuilding, as shown here;

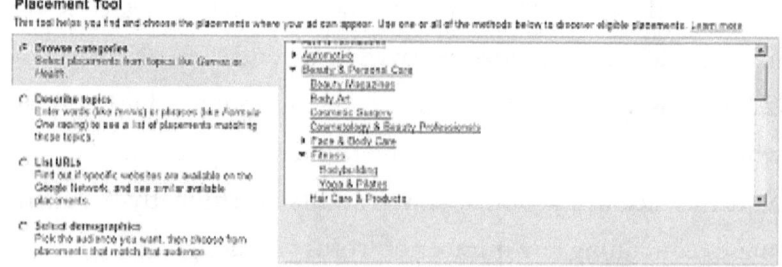

2. Load the home pages of the first 10 sites displayed, then copy-and-paste to copy all of the words on the page to a single Notepad document.

3. Search Google for the term "Bodybuilding Equipment," and copy all of the resulting text into the same Notepad doc.

4. Pull the resultant text file (all 1.5mb of it) into Textanz, and produce a list of the most commonly-occurring 1-word and two-word combinations. Then create a short list of the most frequently-occurring words.

5. Create the final list. Include the negative forms of few words that had appeared frequently - ulcerative and colitis – to ensure that ads don't appear on pages that relate mainly to those terms and aren't relevant to bodybuilding equipment.

The final content-based ad list included bench press, body building, home gym, weight training, fitness, gym, lifting, training, weights, workout, colitis and ulcerative.

Here's another exercise using a B2B company as an example. We'll create ad groups for a fictitious company selling enterprise-level accounting software, BigBeanCounters.com. The CMO at BigBeans has shrewdly deduced that she should create a PPC content campaign to target ads to two kinds of publisher content. The choice of the first group is obvious: sites that discuss/describe the use of enterprise accounting and financial software.

She also decides to target content that is frequented by financial executives at big companies - especially ones who hire internal accountants. Her logic is that the sites' visitors are CFOs and other financial decision-makers -- perfect targets for BigBeans' software. She does a Google search on the terms "enterprise accounting software" and "accounting software for big companies." Then the Textanz software lists the most frequently-occurring one-word and two-word combinations.

The final list includes the words accounting, bigbeancounters, -endocrinology, enterprise accounting, enterprise financial, erp, erp software, financial management, Microsoft dynamics, QuickBooks enterprise, sage software, quicken, small business, -Peachtree software and Microsoft office.

Notice that the list includes a few one-word keywords and many two-word keywords. Always be careful of this fact: the *content-matching algorithms work best with unambiguous keywords*. Put another way: you risk confusing the algorithms with keywords that have several synonyms - more of a danger with one-word keywords than with keywords of two or more words.

So in the example above, the keyword "erp" is safe, because its most common meaning is associated with the expanded acronym, "Enterprise Resource Planning." Having said this, the term is occasionally associated with a medical term, "Endocrinology-Reproductive Physiology." That's why the negative keyword "endocrinology" is included. Doing so tells the algorithm <u>not</u> to display ads on pages that include the term "endocrinology."

I've also included the names of some of BigBeans' competitors: QuickBooks Enterprise and Microsoft Dynamics, for example. So if a page exists that describes/discusses those products, BigBeans' ads will appear on the same page. I've included the negative keyword "Peachtree Software," since that package is used by smaller businesses than my target audience.

The list for the ad groups that targets sites frequented by financial executives who are recruiting accountants includes the keywords for accountant jobs, CFO jobs, enterprise accounting, enterprise financial, enterprise recruitment, finance jobs, recruiting, -army, -navy, -marines, bookkeeper, careerbank, bookkeeping jobs and small business finance.

By now you should be able to figure out why each keyword has been included. The names of American armed forces are included as negative keywords so that the algorithm knows not to place my ads on pages whose content deals with, for example, "army recruiting." Careerbank is included because it's a popular job-listing site for lower-level (i.e., non-enterprise) jobs.

Here are sample ads to match each ad group:

For the Accounting ad group and Recruiting ad group:

Don't Miss a Nickel
Big Company Accounting Software
Saves Time and Money. Free Trial!
www.BigBeanCounters.com

Don't Hire an Accountant
Efficient Software Means Fewer
Employees. Download Our
Whitepaper!
www.BigBeanCounters.com

Notice that both ads feature "soft offers" -- a free trial and a free whitepaper. This acknowledges the fact that readers of content ads are not yet in the buying cycle, so the objective is to ease them into the sales funnel by providing an easy way to get more information. The whitepaper offer is somewhat "softer" than the free trial, in light of the fact that hiring managers are even further from the sales funnel than people who view ads on sites describing accounting software. Creating demand for information is a key step to creating demand for products and services. And demand is the differentiator for content-based advertising.

CHAPTER 4

Using Google Placement

Now you can temporarily dispense with keywords. We're entering the world of Google AdWords, which includes a powerful feature that lets advertisers place ads on specific sites displaying AdSense units. Placement-targeted campaigns (originally called Site Targeted campaigns) consist of ad groups that are identical to ones in traditional content campaigns except for one key attribute: ad groups contain lists of web sites, not keywords.

Placement-targeted ad groups can include all content ad types: text, static and animated graphics in a wide variety of sizes and formats, and even video. Advertisers can choose whether to be charged on a CPM (cost per thousand impressions) or CPC (cost per click) basis. The ability to choose specific sites is powerful, but Google goes it one better. Advertisers can choose to display their ads on specific pages within a site, or even subsections of pages. For example, advertisers can choose to advertise on the

New York Times web site in the business, fashion, health, travel or sports sections - and many more.

Placement-targeted campaigns offer several advantages over keyword-targeted content campaigns. Since a company can target ads to specific sites, it can tailor its ads to appeal specifically to the readers of site groups. For example, an apparel retailer could display travel-clothing-related ads on travel sites or even tailor ads to readers of individual sites. So a soap pad manufacturer could create special ads for the Boston.com sites that say "Beantown Loves Brillo!"

Another big advantage: you can set individual bids for each site. So by running reports that show the CTR and conversion rate data for each site, a company can fine tune each site's maximum CPC to achieve acceptable (or hopefully great) ROI for each site.

And yet another advantage: Placement-targeted text ads get stretched and enlarged to fill an entire ad unit - the mythical, seldom-spotted "expanded text ad." Google describes it as *"an expanded text ad is a text ad that fills an entire ad unit on its own, rather than being grouped with other text ads. Expanded text ads have the same character limits and as typical text ads, but are displayed solo and with text enlarged."*

So if a publisher has specified that a strip of four AdWords ads should appear in a banner at the bottom of a page, Placement-targeted ads will muscle the other ads off the ad unit and be displayed big and bold.

How do advertisers find which web sites display Google AdWords content ads? Google provides the Placement Tool, which selects sites in a variety of ways. Advertisers can browse a list of categories, enter keyword topics, list specific URLs of sites that display AdWords ads, or select sites whose visitors exhibit desired demographic attributes.

In each case the tool digs into the pool of site publishers and lets advertisers choose which sites (or site subsections) will carry the ads. Unfortunately the Placement Tool can be inefficient. It frequently suggests sites that bear no resemblance to the chosen category or topic. Worse, it neglects to show appropriate sites that may be perfect matches.

Demographic Targeting

The great promise of the Internet is the knowledge of who is expected to see an ad, and then knowing who actually interacted with it. Content-based advertising takes this capacity to a new level. Campaigns can be fine-tuned to focus more on sites whose visitors match the advertiser's favored demographic groups. For example, in ContextWeb's content-based ADSDAQ Exchange advertisers are targeting the actual ad pages in which whose content will be most attractive to potential customers. It's a kind of automatic demographic targeting. The demographics of the site and its specific pages reflect the demographic targets of the content campaign.

On Google demographic bidding is available whether you are using contextual or placement targeting and with both CPC and

CPM bidding. Content advertisers can choose to boost their ad group bids by as much as 500 percent for demographic slices that they know to respond better to their ads. At least as important, advertisers can choose to entirely exclude demographic slices to which ads should not be served.

Here's a snapshot from Google Content of the demographic slices that can be controlled:

Gender:

Gender	Impr.	Clicks	CTR	Cost	Make Adjustments	
Male	0	0	0.00%	$0.00	Bid + 0%	Edit
Female	0	0	0.00%	$0.00	Bid + 0%	Edit
Unspecified	0	0	0.00%	$0.00		
Total	0	0	0.00%	$0.00		

Traffic Report by Gender (for last 7 days)

Age:

Age	Impr.	Clicks	CTR	Cost	Make Adjustments	
0-17	0	0	0.00%	$0.00		Edit
18-24	0	0	0.00%	$0.00	Bid + 0%	Edit
25-34	0	0	0.00%	$0.00	Bid + 0%	Edit
35-44	0	0	0.00%	$0.00	Bid + 0%	Edit
45-54	0	0	0.00%	$0.00	Bid + 0%	Edit
55-64	0	0	0.00%	$0.00	Bid + 0%	Edit
65+	0	0	0.00%	$0.00	Bid + 0%	Edit
Unspecified	0	0	0.00%	$0.00		
Total	0	0	0.00%	$0.00		

Traffic Report by Age (for last 7 days)

So for example, if an advertiser's target audience is composed of females from age 18-34, the advertiser can choose to shut off ad delivery for all males, and for females whose age is below and above that range. Bid boosts can be cumulative - so if an advertiser chooses to increase bid prices by 200 percent for males and 300 percent for the age bracket 55-64, then the advertiser will pay up to 500 percent of the ad group base bid price for each click.

Finding More Placement Sites

One way to find sites for placement-targeted ad groups involves using a software tool called Web Data Extractor (www. webextractor.com) that automatically runs search engine queries on search terms you input, and generates a list of sites that feature those terms. Web Data Extractor (WDE) has many other features, but we'll just focus on URL extraction for these examples.

Using the tool is simple: you specify one or more search terms, choose a set of search engines, hit a button and seconds later you have a text file chock full of pertinent web site URLs. Though you can specify more than one search term, it works best using only one per session -- that will make cleaning out junk URLs (described below) easier. You also have the option of specifying only US/International search engines, or select ones from outside the U.S.

We used the tool to find bodybuilding sites -- to create a placement-targeted campaign to augment the keyword-targeted campaign illustrated in Chapter 4. We specified the search term "bodybuilding equipment" (including the quotation marks to tell the software I wanted to see only sites with that exact phrase). Within seconds WDE produced a list of 557 URLs. A quick glance revealed there were some very pertinent sites included -- but also quite a few irrelevant sites, like google.com and youtube. com.

Rather than manually weed out the less-relevant URLs, simply paste the entire list into Google's Placement Tool -- and let the tool tell me which sites accept AdWords ads. From there it was easy to weed out the irrelevant sites. Furthermore, the Placement Tool suggested dozens of additional sites that were similar to the relevant sites.

Just 10 minutes after starting the exercise, the Placement Tool generated a tight list of targeted sites such as criticalbench. com, gain-weight-muscle-fast.com, female-bodybuilders.org, fitnessatlantic.com, one4fitness.com, fitnesspros.com, and more.

An alternative to the steps above would be to manually weed out obviously irrelevant sites, and then past the pared-down list into the placement-targeted ad group via the Edit Placements option. Even if you do it this way, you might want to return to the Placement Tool and paste the list into the "List URLs" box and get available placements – to see whether the tool suggests additional sites that are similar to the list you pasted in.

Other search engines and content-based exchanges such as ADSDAQ employ different placement strategies. For example, ADSDAQ stresses the concept of contextual placement that catches the potential customer during the exploration and discovery phase of the demand creation cycle. I'll cover integration with the rest of the Internet next.

Chapter 5

Integrating With Other Content Networks and Exchanges

Though it may come as a surprise to some Internet marketers (and journalists) Google is not the only search engine or the only option for content-based advertising. Google's content-based tool is on one hand an effective and fast way to find the sites that valuable customers will visit. But all that cutting and pasting can be tedious. For example, using the Google AdWords web interface to build out banner ad campaigns can be a slow, tedious chore.

It's best to learn AdWords Editor to compress the time and effort. This free Google tool makes editing ad groups of any kind a snap. Furthermore, as explained below, AdWords Editor (AWE for short) might be your best friend if you conduct PPC ad campaigns on the "Big Four" - Google, Yahoo, Microsoft and ADSDAQ Exchange by ContextWeb.

First, an AWE overview: it's a standalone software application that downloads the structure and content of an AdWords account to perform fast, easy changes - think Microsoft Excel for AdWords. Use it to perform almost all of the functions done through the AdWords web interface - in a fraction of the time. Two features stand out. First, it enables an advertiser to cut, copy and paste almost any entity -- from a single keyword or ad (text or image) to an entire campaign. Second, advertisers can perform global search and replace operations to change any text -- in keywords and ad copy, for example -- and even bid prices.

Check out these two AWE screen caps, and imagine how you would use them to make fast changes to your campaigns:

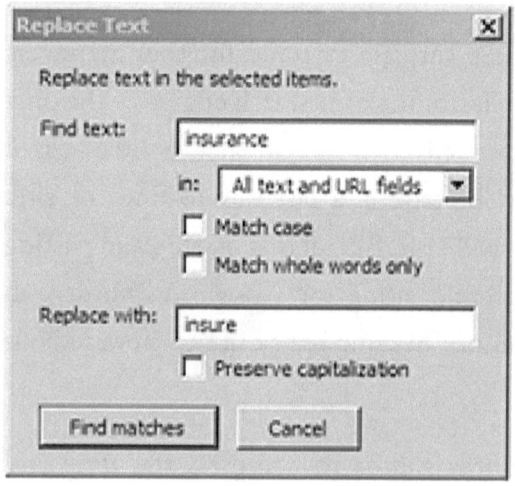

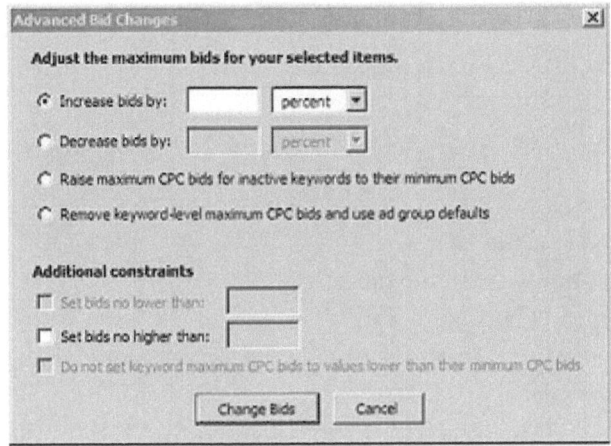

Here's the procedure for splitting ad groups:

1. Highlight the name of the original ad group in AWE.
2. Copy and paste the ad group -- use the menus, or do a quick CTRL-C CTRL-V sequence of keystrokes.
3. Immediately rename the ad group - we've found it useful to include the ad type in the ad group name -- e.g. "Exercise Bikes 720x90"
4. Click on the AWE "Ads" tab, and delete all but the one ad you want to retain.
5. Repeat until all ads are split into ad groups with one ad each. Pause the original ad group and set the new ones to Active.

Time with AWE: 5 minutes. Time through the web interface - at least 30 minutes.

So why is AWE a godsend to Yahoo, Microsoft and ADSDAQ advertisers? Because is lets you export data - entire ad groups or campaigns, for example -- into a standard CSV file that can be used as a bulk upload file to create new ad groups and campaigns in Yahoo! Search Marketing (Panama), Microsoft adCenter and ContextWeb's ADSDAQ Exchange.

Here are the steps for exporting a campaign to Yahoo:

1. In AdWords Editor, go to File, then Export to CSV
2. Save the CSV file
3. Log into Yahoo Search Marketing
4. Click on the Campaign Tab
5. Click on Import (directly under and to the right of the campaign tab)
6. Click on the Convert Third Party Campaigns Tab (in the middle of the page)
7. Upload the CSV file that you exported and saved from AWE

And here are the steps for exporting a campaign to Microsoft:

1. In AdWords Editor, go to File, then Export to CSV
2. Save the CSV file
3. Log into Microsoft adCenter
4. Click on Campaigns
5. Click on Import campaigns
6. Click on Excel (in blue) to download a template
7. Copy and Paste the data from your AdWords Editor file to the template
8. Save the template
9. On MSN, click "Import File"

And finally, the process for importing existing text ads to ADSDAQ is a bit simpler. In fact, while creating an ADSDAQ campaign you can save all the data for future exports.

1. In AdWords Editor, go to File, then Export to CSV
2. Save the CSV file

3. Log into ADSDAQ Buying Desk
4. Go to ad library.
5. Find option to import text ads.
6. Copy and Paste the data from your AdWords Editor file to the template

In each of these cases you may need to make adjustments once the campaigns are uploaded -- to meet ad line length requirements, for example. There's a lot of data to export or import including bid prices, creative, and keywords that were used for search engines. But regardless of those adjustments, there are tools available that make navigating between search engines and ad exchanges doable. Content, as we have said, is the future. And the future is based on cooperation and compatibility.

CHAPTER 6:

Content's New Business Model: Using ContextWeb's ADSDAQ Exchange

The latest addition into the new frontier of content-based advertising is ContextWeb's ADSDAQ Exchange. Do not think of ADSDAQ as a search engine or even an ad network. It is a true exchange that allows publishers to set an asking price, and for advertisers to then bid on their presence on the publisher content pages. Within the ADSDAQ model advertisers don't worry about individual keywords or sites. The advertiser chooses from among approximately 400 categories, and ADSDAQ's exchange places ads on all pages within its exchange that correspond to the chosen category.

Targeting advertising by choosing from among categories is much easier than "backward mapping" categories to keywords, as Google requires. Furthermore, choosing categories allows advertisers to focus more on the "bigger picture" -- identifying

33

target customer sets and the sites that they're likely to frequent. Once again, the goal is creating demand for new customers.

ADSDAQ makes it easy for advertisers to choose categories. First, view all categories and choose from among them with a click of the mouse:

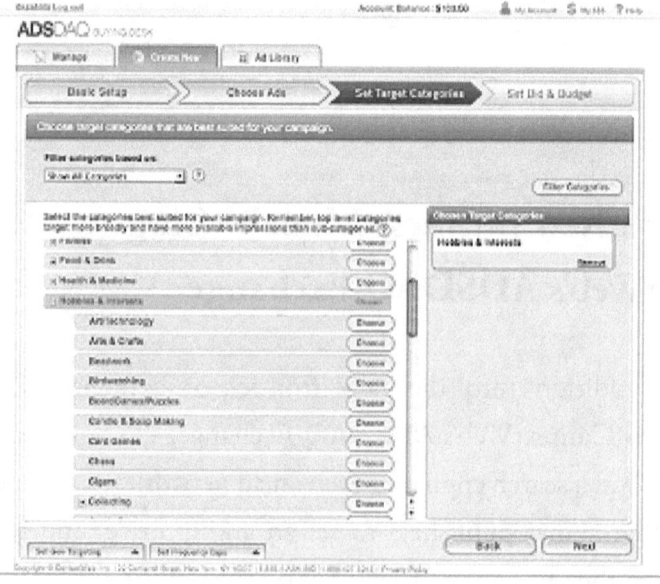

Alternatively, you can enter keywords that describe your product or service -- or the nature of the pages where you want ads to appear -- and ADSDAQ will suggest the categories that are most suitable for your campaign:

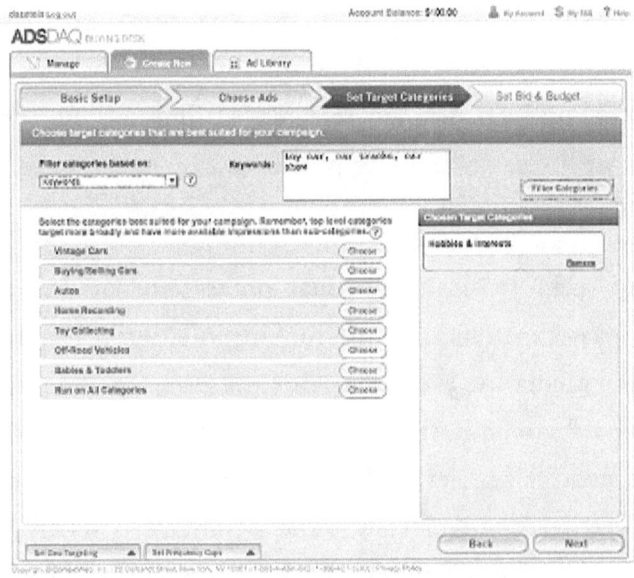

And perhaps easiest of all, enter the URL of any site - your own, or one that's typical of the sites where you want your ads to appear - and ADSDAQ will suggest the most pertinent categories:

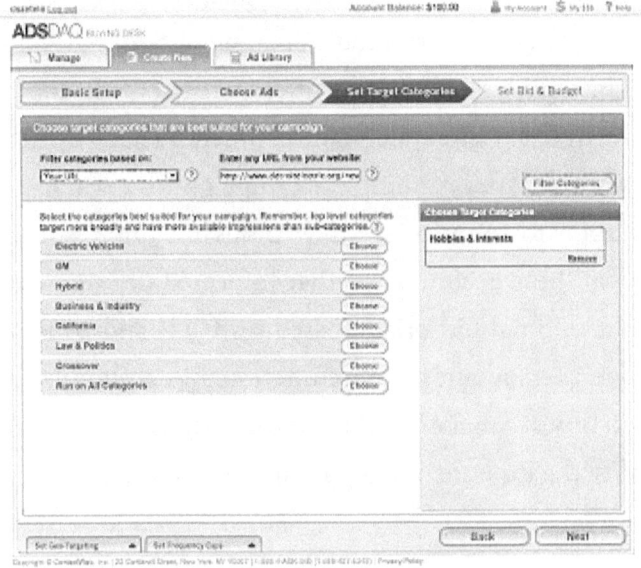

ADSDAQ's ability to target site pages by category is a powerful advantage for advertisers -- there's no guesswork to choose the right keywords, and no detailed research to find specific web sites. And as we'll see, the bidding process is easy to target ROI or branding targets.

Bidding may seem to be an unusual process for marketers, especially if past experience stems from negotiating CPM for banners, print media, or even TV. But the exchange concept requires advertisers to understand bidding, and it is a much better way to understand fair prices, and even spend budgets efficiently from the advertiser point of view. The advantage is relatively straightforward. At the beginning of a new Internet campaign, advertisers usually start slow, planning to pick up the pace when they accumulate enough data upon which to make optimization decisions. Enter the bidding concept. The ideal initial bidding strategy depends on whether you prefer a prudent or aggressive approach. Prudent advertisers should assume a minimal CTR and conversion rate -- say, .05 percent-.1 percent CTR and .5 percent-1 percent conversion rate -- and estimate a relatively high impression volume. After running the campaign for a while – at least long enough to see at least a few thousand impressions - enough data will have accumulated that informed decisions can be made about optimal bid prices, based on CTR and/or ROI. Aggressive advertisers might be more interested in accumulating data quickly in order to make optimization decisions earlier -- and therefore justify the expense of a higher minimum bid price.

ADSDAQ provides more guidance than Google on starting bid prices. During campaign setup or anytime thereafter, ADSDAQ shows you a bid range and allows you to choose any click price within that range.

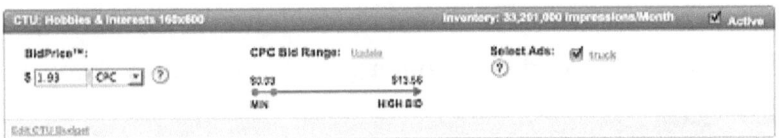

The low end of the range indicates approximately how much publishers want to be paid, while the high end indicate how much your competitors are willing to pay. If you've been following this book's advice so far, you may now be running ad groups that include a mix of text and non-text ads. If so, take a look at the performance data, and you will probably see that the performance metrics for each ad type may be widely different.

We've seen CTR and conversion rate differences as high as 500 percent from one ad to another. The root cause may be obvious in the case of text ads vs. non-text ads, but we've also seen wide variations between non-text ads of different configurations. Skyscraper banners can have higher CTRs than horizontal banners, for example. This kind of variance makes it challenging to set minimum bid prices. So the best practice is to isolate each ad type/configuration into its own ad group. This not only lets you set bid prices to achieve target ROI, it also allows you to more easily test ad variations.

ADSDAQ places ads based on the effective CPM of the advertiser. For example, let's say Advertiser One bids a $4 CPC and gets a 0.05 percent CTR for an effective CPM of $2. Advertiser Two bids $2 and gets a 0.2 percent CTR for an effective CPM of $4; Advertiser Three bids a $5 CPC and gets a 0.2 percent CTR for an effective CPM of $10. Based on the formula, the ADSDAQ Exchange will rank these in order of advertiser Three, Two, and then One.

Google's system is different, in that Google wants to reward advertisers who present ads that are optimally relevant to people who perform Google searches, and who "land" PPC-driven site visitors on pages that are relevant to the searcher's intent and the promise of the ad. It calculates a "Quality Score," and rewards well-behaved advertisers by making it possible for their ads to achieve better ad position than competitors who may be bidding and paying more per click. Though on the surface Google AdWords Search Quality Score (QS) can seem complicated, it's actually pretty straightforward, since the Google algorithms have plenty of textual context (keyword lists, text ad copy, landing page content) to judge whether an ad campaign is relevant to the search terms included in the ad group.

The Google system is simple when you understand that the *content ad group quality score is based almost entirely on CTR (click-through-rate).* This becomes intuitively obvious when you consider the case of non-text content ads in placement-targeted campaigns. Since the advertiser lists domain names instead of keywords, there's zero keyword context. Since the ads are graphical instead of text, there's zero ad-copy context. So there's no way for a content-matching algorithm to judge the relevancy of an ad group to a landing page - and landing page content can't possibly influence QS.

Advertisers should consider the aggressive approach when placing content-based campaigns whether it's through Google or ADSDAQ. Unlike search campaigns that have to be optimized, time is not on your side with content-based ads. It's better to start bids high, effectively "buying CTR," and then move bids lower once the best categories and content pages have been determined. Of course, creating effective ads that garner maximum CTR must be a key part of this strategy.

Content-based ad campaigns also require a mind shift when considering results. CTR for most campaigns means "click-through rate." But because customer acquisition is the goal here, advertisers should think in terms of "customer acquisition to campaign ratio." Every click for a content-based ad is a potential customer. At the end of the day, the number of new customers is the measurement that matters and all other measurements have an impact on that ratio.

CHAPTER 7

Writing Effective Text Ads

As we have mentioned several times, content-based advertising is not a quest for the perfect set of keywords or the ultimate search engine optimization strategy. It is about customers, now. No matter how good your content-based advertising is, the information on the page your ad is featured on is the focal point for every visitor and potential customer. Your advertising is peripheral; tangential to the main attraction. So just like traditional print advertising, your ads need to work hard to get noticed. It's not a search engine result page. The ad must distract the reader's attention *away* from the "articles" and *toward* the ads.

How do print advertisers do that? Eye-catching graphics. Headlines that are controversial. Outrageous promises.

How can you design ads that grab the site visitor's attention? Try these:

Scream. Think loud. Your ads can, and should, shout their way off the screen. Don't be afraid to be borderline obnoxious – it works for "Head On" (Apply Directly to the Forehead!) and many other advertisers. You can afford to be much more disruptive than you are in your search ads. One important reason: Quality Score doesn't count. The only number that counts, is the click thru rate, which is the most important element of your effective CPM, CTR. Since keywords don't trigger bold words in your ads (as they do in search ads) you can use anything you like in your headlines. The more eye-catching, the better.

Bribe. Remember, the ad reader is at the beginning – or before – the sales cycle. They need a strong incentive to proceed. Free offers – free downloads, free shipping, free trials – work well. If you're a B2B advertiser, seeking leads – bribe readers with a free whitepaper. B2C advertisers can give free samples. Loyalty clubs can give free points. And so on.

Stand Apart. Your ads are competing with the web page's content – and also with the other ads on the page – usually 3-4 other ads in addition to yours. So your ad needs to distract attention away from the page content <u>and</u> the competing ads – no mean feat. So even more than in Search, study your competition's ads and make sure yours are different – preferably louder.

Get Imperative. Our testing has shown that imperatives in headlines and body copy work well to get attention. Words like Stop! Wait! Look! attract the eye as assuredly as if the reader heard them shouted.

Be Emotional: Appeal to the reader's most basic emotions. For example, people hate to believe they're missing something important. Tell them what they'll miss or fail to achieve if they don't click on your ad. Or take a cue from the insurance companies and scare'em – tell them about the dire circumstances they'll experience if they fail to click.

Hopefully you're getting the picture: shy, understated, soft-selling content ads don't work. They quietly beg to be ignored. The good news is that it's not hard for you to write ads that pop off the page and get results.

Good Search Ad ≠ Good Content Ad

Let's compare bad and good Search ads, and then look at an example of a good Content ad.

Search ad A is typical of many you'll see in the search listings. Simple lists of what's being sold. No competitive advantages, no benefits, no calls to action. No clicks.

    A. Bad Search Ad:

<u>Outdoor Furniture</u>
Tables, chairs, lounges.
Wood and plastic.
www.franksfurniture.com

    Search ad B employs some of the Search ad best practices:

- Capital letters in the body copy and the display URL
- Benefits (the word "durable")

- A call to action
- An extra word in the display URL that corresponds to the search term

B. Better Search Ad:

Outdoor Furniture
Durable Patio Beauty. See
Low Prices on Top Brands!
www.FranksFurniture.com/Outdoor

Content ad C demonstrates some of the stand-out best practices I described earlier -- an eye-catching headline that appeals to base emotions.

C. Even Better Content Ad:

Dazzle the Neighbors
But Don't Tell Them about Our Low
Deck Furniture Prices. Buy Now!
www.FranksFurniture.com/Outdoor

Next I'll reflect on the best ad copywriting practices I described above, and give specific examples. Remember, in Content advertising, your ads can and should:

Scream. Remember, you're competing with web page content. Your ads need to leap loudly off the screen. Grab attention with emotionally-charged words like this:

Your Online Ads Failing?
Discover How To Reach Your Target
Request Your Live Demo Today!
www.ADSDAQ.com

Bribe. Since the ad reader is at the beginning -- or before -- the sales cycle, it's often a good idea to offer them something for free -- a sample, a no-obligation trial -- to get them onto your site and taking an action. Here's an example:

Free CRM Software
Keep Customers Happier.
Download Free Trial Today!
www.HappyCustomers.com/CRM

Stand Apart. Since your ads need to distinguish themselves from the page content and with the other ads on the page, it often helps to catch the eye and dare to compare yourself to your competitors -- like this:

AdWords Alternative
Cut Your Costs & Your Time
Get Your Live Demo Today!
www.ADSDAQ.com

Get Imperative. Imperative words and phrases like "Stop!" and "Look!" make site visitors... well... stop and look. They attract the eye the way the shouted words would attract the ear:

<u>Don't Take Vacation</u>
Wait! Avoid a Bad Trip.
Buy Travel Insurance.
www.TripCoverage.com

Be Emotional: Appealing to reader's basic emotions is a tactic that's been used in print, TV and radio ads for years -- because doing so evokes strong images that attract attention, even amidst distractions. For example, we've had a lot of success with scare tactics like this:

<u>Is Your Dog Dying?</u>
You'll never know unless
you ask these 5 vet questions.
www.PetPills.com

Testing... Testing...

Now that you see how much latitude advertisers have with content ad copy, here's one more piece of advice: just as in Search, smart advertisers continually test their ad copy. The easiest way to do this is to run a/b split testing -- two ads served in rotation (being sure to switch campaign settings from "Optimize" to "Rotate" to make sure they run in true rotation). ADSDAQ automatically drops pages or categories that don't perform and therefore calculates the performance of creative on those pages. Another reason to test ads: there may be an "ad fatigue" effect that takes place over time -- click-through-rates may drop over time because frequent site visitors may become less reactive when they've seen the same ad repeated over and over. One possible solution might be to switch periodically between two top-performing ads.

Testing and improving ad copy is essential to optimizing overall PPC campaign performance. Improving ad text results in more people clicking on your ad (higher click-through-rate, or CTR) and can also improve conversion rates. In Google AdWords, ad testing and optimization leads to better CTR and quality score, which means it can help drive your CPC down, and/ or let you buy more clicks per dollar. So it has a direct impact on your campaign's ability to increase the number of profitable sales. In ADSDAQ, better ad copy will lead to a higher CTR or interaction rate with the ad, which will allow ADSDAQ to run the effective creative more frequently on the targeted pages you have requested.

It's important for you to understand the valid ways to measure and compare ad performance. The following example illustrates this. I'll compare two ads, A and B below.

Here's ad version A:

Industrial Widgets
Top Widgets for Industrial
Use. Fast, FREE Shipping!
WidgetsRUS.com/Industrial+Widgets

And here's ad version B:

Green Widgets
Durable, Earth-friendly.
Fast, FREE Shipping!
WidgetsRUS.com/Green+Widgets

Here's the performance data for ads A and B:

Ad Version	Impressions	Clicks	CTR	Avg CPC
A	12,913	1,058	8.19%	$0.95
B	50,523	2,767	5.48%	$1.22

Cost	Conversions	Conversion Rate	Cost/ Conversion
$1,003.86	118	11.15%	$8.51
$3,389.06	270	9.76%	$12.55

Assume that the landing page for this ad contains multiple design elements - graphics and words - whose main message is that Widgets "R" Us features industrial widgets at lower prices than its competitors. Assume also that the target maximum cost per conversion is $9.00, and that the campaign needs to be managed tightly to that number.

So what does the performance data show us? It seems ad A is the clear "winner." Its CTR, 8.19 percent, is significantly higher than ad B's 5.48 percent. Furthermore, ad A's cost per conversion is lower than the target $9.00, while average cost per conversion for ad B is almost $4.00 more than the target.

The correct action to take is to pause Ad B, and write a variation of Ad A with changes that you think might improve performance. How frequently should you make ad optimization changes? Our simple rule of thumb is: you shouldn't make a decision about whether to judge ad winners and losers, until the ad group has accumulated at least 30-100 clicks and 30-100 conversions.

The exact number of clicks and conversions necessary to make decisions depends on the velocity of your ad groups. If your ad group accumulates clicks and conversions quickly (say, hundreds or thousands of clicks and conversions per day), you should use the high end of that range. If the ad group accumulates clicks and conversions more slowly -- hundreds of clicks and conversions per month, for example -- then you should use the low end of each range.

Purists might say that 30 clicks or conversions are too little data to make decisions based on statistical validity. While that's indisputable, for many advertisers it's simply impractical to wait the weeks or even months before enough data accumulates. Certainly there's a risk that an incorrect decision will be made -- e.g. an ad might be shut off that might perform well if left to run for a longer time. But for many advertisers, that risk is outweighed by the risk of failing to make any decision.

Performance Troubleshooting and Optimization

PROBLEM	SOLUTION
Low Number of Impressions	• Increase bid prices • Increase the number of categories (ADSDAQ) • Increase the number of sites (Google)
Low click-through-rate (CTR)	• Improve ad copy • Exclude sites (Google) • Test alternative categories (ADSDAQ)
Low conversion rates	• Improve landing pages • Improve ad copy
High cost-per-conversion (CPA)	• Lower bid prices • Improve ads (Google) • Improve landing pages

CHAPTER 8

Beyond Text: Adding Graphical Ads to Content

Text and content go together logically. But content-based advertising is not limited to text. It's time to step out of your comfort zone and face an exciting possibility: Content-based advertising can be more than just text -- there are many more ad media available to contextual advertisers. In fact, static graphic banners, animated banners (GIFs and Flash) and video ads are all in the content ad toolkit. Let's start our discussion of non-text ads by focusing on the ads themselves. Reflect back to the last chapter that described best practices for text ads for the content network; the same rules apply to non-text ads.

First, the ad must distract the attention of the site visitor *away from* the main reason they visited the site: the page content. So the ad needs to be eye-catching enough to stand out from the page. This is a particularly big challenge these days, given the possibility that web site visitors as a whole may have developed "banner fatigue," gliding right over graphic ads on their way to their precious content.

That's the reason you see so many "dancing babies" and "bop the mole" ads - eye-catching (and sometimes bizarre) motion catches the eye. Once the eye has been caught, the real work begins: getting the click. The non-text ad needs to work hard and fast to convince the potential site visitor that there's a strong reason to click on the ad.

So the ad needs to telegraph these concepts in rapid succession:

1. "This ad's for me" - usually via a connection to the page's subject matter
2. There's a reason for me to look closely at the ad (features and benefits)
3. Pre-qualification (optional) - make sure the wrong people aren't persuaded to click
4. Pre-sale (optional) - describe the action you want them to take on the landing page
5. Call to action (e.g. "Start Saving Now!)

Let's take a look at a sampling of banner ads and see how well they convey these messages. First up is this ad from Marketbright, a company that specializes in lead generation programs for businesses.

The ad has one main strength: a clear call to action, in the form of the "Click Here!" button, in the bottom center of the ad unit. That's perfect button placement, since studies show that's where the eye usually ends up after tracking down through the ad from the upper left.

The ad is also strong in its challenge to potential customers ("are you ready?") and its call to action below the click button. By clicking, the ad promises you will convert contacts to customers. It is weaker in other respects: first, unless the ad appears on sites specifically related to generating new customers there's only a slim connection between the ad's first main message and site content (I found the ad on a page related to tech gadget news). Second, the background of the ad (an empty sky) doesn't necessarily call to mind new customers or the revenue to be gained from them.

Let's move on to one of my favorites: this LowerMyBills.com ad.

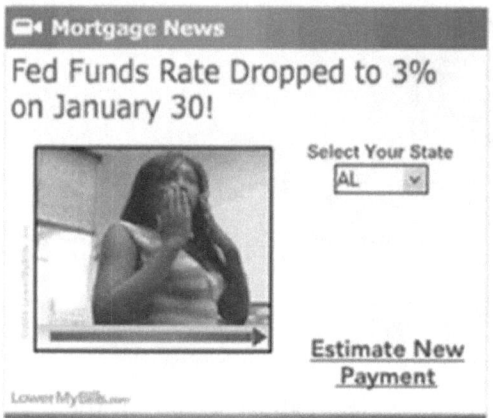

The animated version of the ad shows a grainy amateur video of two women dancing in an office setting. One of them whirls towards the camera and is embarrassed to be caught in such an un-businesslike act. The graphic obviously doesn't relate at all to the selling point of the ad, but since people seem to enjoy witnessing others' embarrassment, it's hard not to get engaged in the video. There's even a "replay" button, which I suspect is used pretty often.

The "Fed Funds Rate Dropped..." message is not particularly strong, but it becomes clear pretty quickly that there's a strong possible benefit. The call to action is clear and easy: select your state and click on the "Estimate New Payment" link, nicely presented as a standard underlined hyperlink.

Here's a weaker ad. Try to figure out what's being sold.

The ad telegraphs a benefit that can be motivating: the $9.99 price. But it's too difficult to figure out what's being sold and why I should buy it. Is it a plate full of olives? Is it two plates (including the mysterious object in the lower left)?

All in all, it's a weak ad with washed-out colors and even a wasted opportunity. On the right side of the banner, where the eye rests after the traverse from left to right, the valuable real estate that should contain a strong call to action instead features a confusing logo that fails to motivate.

Let's finish up with this winner from Colorado Technical University:

First, the overall design suggests a college diploma at first glance, which should attract/distract the eye of people interested in getting a master's degree. The benefit is clear and compelling -- what master's degree candidate wouldn't want to look into an opportunity to be finished with the whole thing in less than a year and a half?

I especially like the call to action, which simultaneously reinforces a powerful motivator: selfishness. "You Owe it to Yourself" flashes at the bottom left, attracting the eye with a message that's somewhat of a non sequitur, but one that's apt to receive a reaction of, "Hell yes I do!" The button simultaneously provides the action mechanism and sets up the pre-sale by telling customers what they should do when they click through to the site.

The Three Commandments of Graphical Ads:

1. Capture Attention. As much as possible make sure the ad captures the attention of the page visitor. If your campaign is working well, the content of the ad will match the content on the page so make sure it is eye catching and disruptive enough to stand out from the content and intrigue the customer beyond the page content.

2. Call to Action. Include a clear call to action. When it comes to creating customer demand you want customers to learn more. So make sure the ad gives them a promise for more information, or a special offer if they click through to a web page or register for more information. More often than not demand creation involves information and attention. Make sure your ad asks for both.

3. Compelling Value. Illustrate clear and compelling value: No ad should be too far from the value offered by your product or service. If it's a great vacation spot, make sure that's front and center. If it's a quality education, don't mince that.

Chapter 9

Landing Pages: Who Are Your Customers and Where Are They Going?

Now let's talk a little bit about where those customers are going after they see an ad or better yet, click on it. Landing pages have more impact on conversion rates and ROI than anything else they can do. And the few truly analytics-obsessed advertisers don't stop at landing pages. They build, test and optimize the entire conversion path, from the landing page through the last page of the conversion process.

Here are some simple concepts to embrace. First, what's a pay-per-click Landing Page? It's simply a page on your site that is customized to match the theme of a particular PPC ad group -- the keywords and ad message. Which brings us to an important point. *The PPC Landing Page can, and often should, look very different from the other pages on your site.*

This is often a difficult but crucial concept that's hard for many site owners to grasp. They're accustomed to thinking about their site as analogous to a bricks-and-mortar storefront: one entrance (the home page) through which all customers enter, linked to other pages where site visitors can (hopefully) easily find what they're looking for. Site owners often design their home page to satisfy the needs of casual browsers as well as visitors who are looking for specific items or information.

This design viewpoint makes sense when the source of site traffic is natural search or links from other sites, since it's difficult to know or infer the visitor's need/intent. But with a properly-constructed PPC campaign, the advertiser knows with laser-beam precision, by virtue of the content-based parameters and the ad message that elicited the click, the visitor's need and intent.

Let's pause for an alternative metaphor. Most sites are not like a storefront with a single entrance. Think of a circular building with multiple entrances. Signs around each entrance describe the products sold just inside the door. The customer who walks through the door sees only the products described by the outside signage. It's easy for customers to find what they're looking for, and they can conduct their transaction quickly and easily.

There's a real-world example of this: Sears stores. Most have multiple entrances, and often those entrances are labeled to indicate which department is just inside the door. The guy who enters the hardware department door doesn't care that Sears also sells baby clothing. He can spend his precious time in the one department that interests him, find what he needs, and finish his transaction quickly.

What if Sears had only one door? Customers would be frustrated by the necessity to wander around the store trying to find the right department. They would be assaulted by the sights and sounds of thousands of products that don't remotely interest them. Some would be distracted from their initial goal, run out of time and leave before buying anything.

You may be thinking, "Some people love to shop. They're actually attracted by the need/opportunity to browse through multiple departments. So the one-door metaphor might be perfect for them." Absolutely true. But thanks to the miracle of modern merchandising, your web site can be like the Sears store with multiple entrances -- and satisfy the needs/desires of the casual shoppers as well as the focused ones.

Most PPC landing pages should be designed with the multiple-entrance metaphor in mind. PPC keywords represent the intent/desire of the shopper. PPC ads are analogous to the signs around each of the multiple entrances -- describing what's inside the entrance, and the benefits the visitor can enjoy. The PPC landing page is like the shoppers experience once they step inside the door.

Which leads us to another important point. *The first and most important objective of the landing page is to convince the visitor that they've come to the right place.* If this crucial first step doesn't happen -- immediately -- many (and possibly most) visitors will hit the back button and click on one of your competitor's ads.

Landing page designers should assume that most people visiting the site via PPC suffer from Attention Deficit Disorder. They're rushing through their day with the usual thousands of distractions, trying to accomplish a task quickly: buy what your site is offering. They see your ad on a web site and click on it. Once your landing page has loaded (hopefully before they've lost patience), they start at the top left corner of the page and try to decide whether the page (and by extension, the site) matches their need/desire. If they conclude it does, they continue scanning the page, and possibly convert. If not, they're gone -- possibly forever.

The Five Commandments of Landing Page Design

1. Small logo. Keep the logo small. Take a look at the landing pages of prominent retailers - the size of the logo has shrunk steadily over the years. I personally believe the logo need be no larger than 200 or so pixels wide by 50 high.

2. Use bullets. Most people, including "ADD" site visitors, don't read content formatted as paragraphs. Put your content - benefits, features - into short, bulleted items.

3. Small Graphics. Graphics can be very helpful -- product photos, pictures of happy people benefitting from your products/services -- but keep the graphics relatively small. They should reinforce your textual messages and help guide the visitor to a quick conversion.

4. Big "next step" button. The button or link that allows the visitor to take the next step in the conversion process should be big, prominent and "above the fold" - visible on the screen without forcing the visitor to scroll to see it.

5. Few links. Limit or exclude off-page navigation. The more specific the search term, the less likely it is that the visitor arrived on your page without conversion intent. For that reason, pages we design often contain only three links - the link going to the next step in the conversion process, plus one each for the Privacy Policy and About Us pages. The latter are included for those visitors who need to feel the site and company are trustworthy. But we want to keep the visitor on the landing page - so we usually open a new window to display these two, leaving the landing page visible and accessible behind.

So what's the best way to ensure visitors conclude they've come to the right place? Reinforce it using the communications medium they've already used: words. You'll improve conversion rates significantly by doing just one thing: mirroring the language of the PPC ad in the area just below the landing page logo. So if the ad is promising "red Nike sneakers," and the ad text includes "Free Shipping. Delivery by Christmas!", the headline below the logo should be "Buy Red Nike Sneakers. Free Shipping and Guaranteed Delivery by Christmas!"

Remember that content-based advertising is creating demand and finding customers. It's not simply harvesting the demand created from the sum total of all the parts of an ad campaign.

Make sure the landing page continues to consider that demand creation.

Logo   Trust Symbols

Headline Mirroring Ad Concept / Promise

Illustration

▸ **Bulleted**

▸ **Benefits**

▸ **Three**

▸ **Four**

**Action Link
(often button)**

Links: Privacy Policy | About Us

Chapter 10

Reporting and Measuring Content Advertising Performance

In this chapter I'll describe important reporting capabilities that give advertisers perfect insight into how well Google and ADSDAQ ad campaigns are performing -- and show you how to use report info to further fine-tune your content campaigns. For AdWords content network advertisers, the most important report is called the Placement Performance Report (PPR), and it lists the sites Google has chosen to display your content ads. For ADSDAQ, the reports come via a Category Impressions Report and an Account Management Report. They generate a gold mine of information, and certainly rival the reports available via keyword search.

To run a PPR on Google simply choose Reports and Create Reports from the AdWords web interface, and then select Placement Performance from the list of Report Types. You can then choose the level of detail to include -- choose Ad Group if you have more than one content ad group per campaign, or Campaign if you have only one ad group per any number of Campaigns.

You can also choose to view just the domain name of the site displaying your ads, or the exact URL of each page displaying the ad. Start by choosing just the domain names, since interpreting performance data will be easier. You can choose any time interval -- but keep in mind that Google started accumulating placement data on June 1, 2007, so you won't be able to generate reports for any dates prior to that.

Underneath the Date Range setting, you'll see an option to report on all campaigns and ad groups, or to select specific ones. You can choose any campaign, despite the fact that only content campaigns will be reported on. First, notice that you have a list of all sites where your ads are appearing. Ignore the rows containing the words "Domain" and "Error page" for now. Notice that you have valuable performance data for each domain: number of impressions, number of clicks, average cost-per-click (CPC), average cost-per-impression (CPM), total cost for the time period specified, and (if you're tracking conversion data -- which you should), number of conversions, conversion rate and cost per conversion.

First thing to check: the length of the domain list. The optimal number of sites will vary depending on the specificity of your ad/product/offer. But here's a rule of thumb: if the number of sites is small - say, fewer than 10 - then your content campaign is probably targeted too narrowly. You may need to use fewer negative keywords, or increase your ad group's bid price to merit appearing on more sites.

More commonly, the list of domains will be very long - from dozens of sites to hundreds. Often this means your ads are appearing on many inappropriate sites - ones whose subject matter bears no relation to your ad/product/service. This is bad news - as discussed in chapters, the main reason that content campaigns perform so poorly (in terms of poor click-through-rates and conversion rates) is that advertiser ads wind up displayed on inappropriate pages.

For most advertisers, the most important data will be conversion data. Google's reports make it easy to see conversion data for campaigns, ad groups, and ads, for any time interval you specify. Here's an example:

Domain	Impressions	Clicks	CTR	Avg CPC	Cost	Conversions	Conversion Rate	Cost / Conversion
kaboodle.com	13755	140	1.02%	1.02	143.12	3	2.14%	47.71
gmail.com	143694	191	0.13%	1.96	374.67	3	1.57%	124.89
about.com	8403	39	0.46%	1.72	67.1	2	5.13%	33.55
Error pages	702	44	6.27%	1.1	48.3	2	4.55%	24.15
sciencedaily.com	6518	17	0.26%	2.15	36.62	1	5.88%	36.62
metafilter.com	161	5	3.11%	1.03	5.14	1	20.00%	5.14

The PPR report gives you the information you need to adjust and optimize your campaign to obtain better and better results. For example, the data above shows that Gmail.com delivered 3 conversions at a cost per conversion of $124.89 -- which could indicate that the advertiser should stop displaying ads on Gmail, or perhaps move Gmail.com into a placement-targeted campaign, so that bid price could be decreased below the $1.96 CPC that resulted in the high-priced conversions. Similarly, the site metafilter.com seems to have the potential to deliver conversions at a low cost-per-conversion -- so that site could likewise be moved into a separate placement-targeted campaign, where this bid for that site could be increased over the current $1.03 CPC.

ADSDAQ advertisers have it easier than Google advertisers. It's worth repeating here that advertisers first pick a category on ADSDAQ and then receive the best web pages automatically. Ads appear on specific pages within the ADSDAQ Exchange on publisher sites, so advertisers don't need to worry about their ads appearing on irrelevant sites or pages. The ADSDAQ system automatically picks the best pages within advertiser-specified categories.

ADSDAQ advertisers can get reports with crucial CTR and conversion data available by campaign, category, or creative. Advertisers can then decide how to adjust campaign parameters -- by excluding categories, for example, or adjusting bid prices. Here's an example of a report sorted by category:

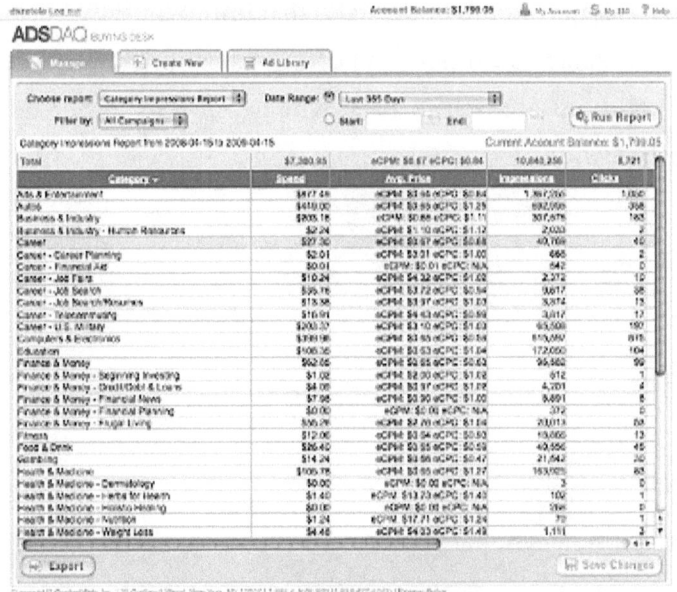

And then a campaign report.

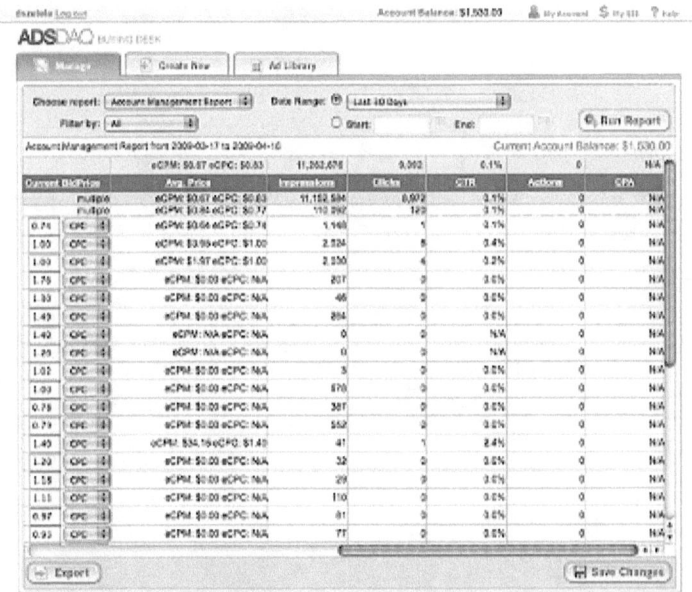

As always it is important to understand that improving advertising performance depends on good reporting capabilities. Content-based ad solutions are rich in data, which will lead to our next topic: optimization.

CHAPTER 11

Optimizing Content Campaigns

Optimizing any ad campaign, or any kind of marketing activity for that matter, comes down to what to leave in and what to leave out. Companies want to do more of what works, and cut their losses on what doesn't as soon as possible.

For many advertisers Internet marketing comes down to three letters: ROI – return on investment. With content-based advertising a company starts from a more predictable ROI playing field than most media can provide. A print campaign is hard to test and harder to measure. Spot TV can be tough on the budget and even tougher on the ROI police in the finance department. Content-based campaigns begin when a company has some kind of idea what kind of customer they want to target. The difference between buying search keywords and content sites is the customer lifecycle. Search catches customers at the end. Content finds them at the beginning.

Both Google and ADSDAQ make optimization easy. Google's Placement Performance Report (as we discussed in the last chapter) is key to exposing poorly-performing sites. Most obvious are those sites that garner a significant number of clicks without delivering conversions. Less obvious are those sites that are delivering few or no clicks and no conversions - but many impressions. These may be harming your ad group's Quality Score, which in term may be adversely affecting your ad rank and/or your average CPC.

On Google, start the optimization project by launching the Site and Category Exclusion Tool from the Tools tab in AdWords. You'll see a screen like this:

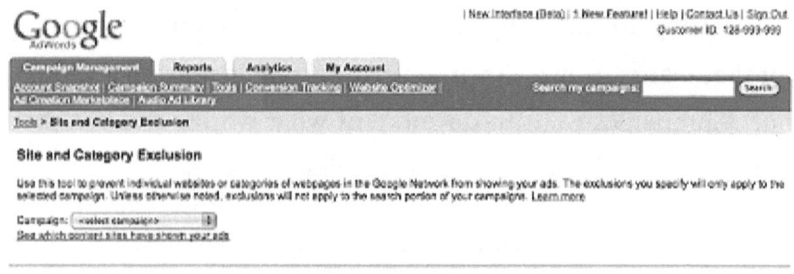

Choose one of your content campaigns. Note that for some reason the tool will allow you to choose non-content campaigns as well; as far as I can tell, trying to exclude sites from search campaigns does effectively nothing.

After choosing a content campaign, you'll see a text entry box like this:

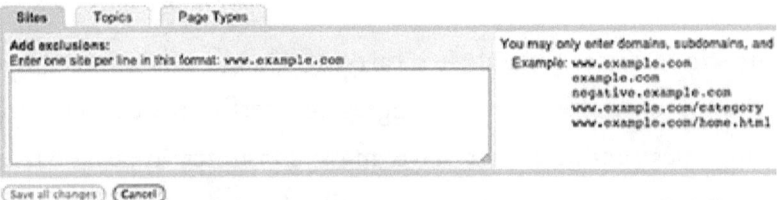

Enter domains in the box and click on "Save All Changes."

You can also exclude certain websites and page types by clicking on the other two tabs:

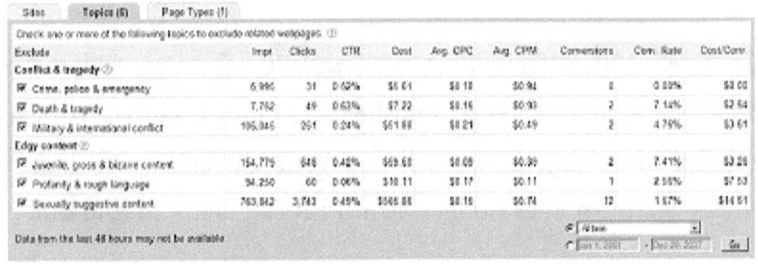

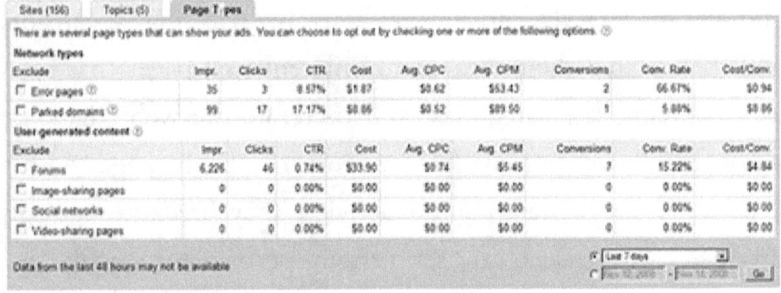

Tips On Google Content Optimization

Voracious Sites: Several sites carrying Google ads attract huge volumes of traffic that, in aggregate, perform well only for companies/products that have mass consumer appeal. Many advertisers will want to avoid these sites from the outset. Two are myspace.com and youtube.com.

Microsurgery: You can generate PPRs that show specific subdirectories and even pages where your ads have appeared. You can then use the Site Exclusion Tool to exclude only subdirectories and pages. This may be overkill, though, unless you're dealing with sites with huge volumes of traffic.

Vote Early, Vote Often: The persistent PPC advertiser will want to run PPRs frequently. New publisher sites join the Google AdSense program every day. Some will run your ads and you'll benefit. Others will burn your budget. Run PPRs regularly to find out.

ADSDAQ does not have site exclusion because it doesn't have to. It looks at advertiser placement and performance at the more granular page level. Advertisers start by selecting a category and then match their content to different web pages that carry that content. The categories, and therefore the web pages, are automatically optimized. If a category or certain pages within a category are generating no activity, they are automatically dropped. Advertisers can set certain performance goals that customize this automated capability. For example, a threshold of cost per acquisition can be set at $40. Therefore, more expensive page inventory would be dropped, eliminating the need for the advertiser to do this manually. ADSDAQ's algorithm constantly examines every page and domain that serves the content that matches the advertiser's goals. When a page or domain fails to perform, your ad is no longer served.

Even though an advanced level automatic optimization comes as standard equipment on ADSDAQ, there are options for further optimization. The first is by bid price. As seen in the screen below, ADSDAQ advertisers can access each campaign by category through the Buying Desk. This campaign is split by "advertising" and "internet technology." The bid range on the CPC for the advertising category is .32 cents at minimum, and the advertiser holds the high bid of $1.40. However, what if the same textual campaign could be run for less money per click? Advertisers can bid lower to try to save money, or bid higher to gain a better foothold on the relevant pages that match their content.

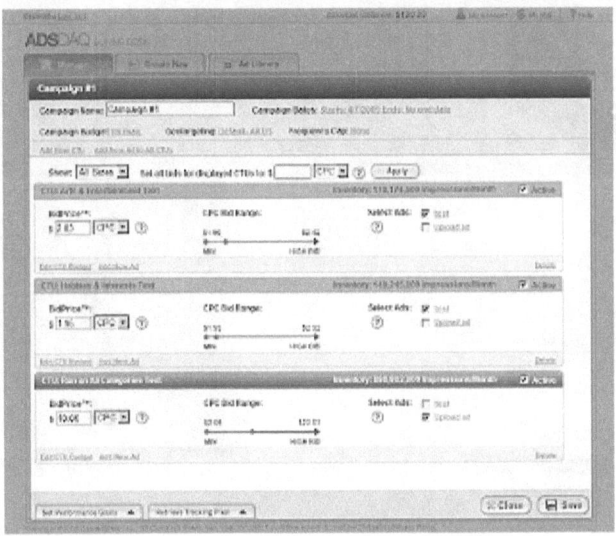

ADSDAQ can also be optimized by performance goals. The image below shows another buying desk tool that sets new thresholds for auto-managed campaign. In addition to the bid range per click illustrated above, the performance goals tab allows optimized CTRs and cost-per-acquisition metrics. Suppose the current CTR of the above-referenced "advertising" category campaign was tracking at a steady 2 percent. Raising the goal to 3 percent would instruct the ADSDAQ algorithm to drop the categories that delivered less, because the rules to define "successful" have been changed by the advertiser. CPA presents a similar opportunity. If new customers are more expensive than the original budgets allowed for, the CPA can be revised down (or up).

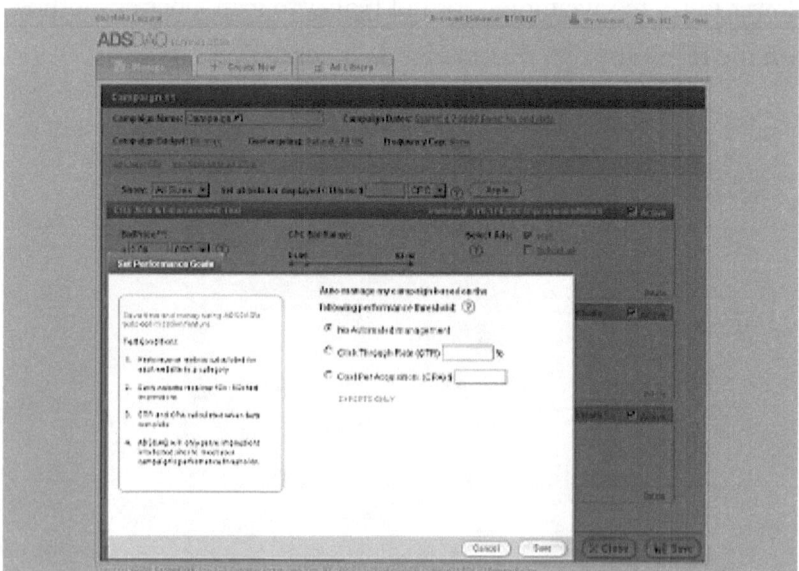

Finally, ContextWeb's ADSDAQ Exchange allows settings for tracking pixels, which connects to the all important "click to action" timeframe. This is one of the edgier features of ADSDAQ and bears indulgence in some quick background. A tracking pixel (also known as a "web bug") is a small image on a web page that permits the loading of the web page to be tracked by a web server. Tracking pixels are also used in HTML email and are the best way to know whether an email has been opened by the intended recipient.

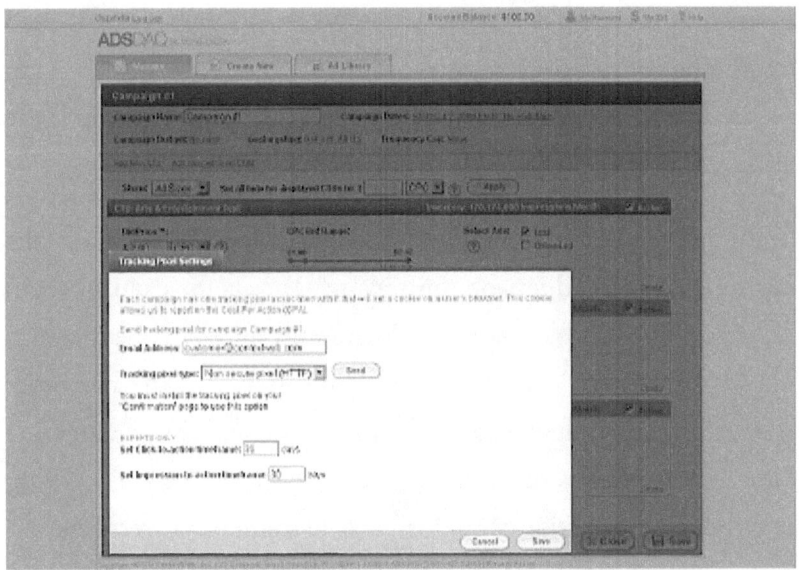

Here's why they're important to ADSDAQ. As illustrated above, the Buying Desk also allows tracking pixels to be sent and controlled. It enables laser-like tracking on the cost-per-action. You can also see that the time that the pixel "lives" on the campaigns' web pages and inboxes can be adjusted. In order to understand this, it's essential to understand the concept of the "click to action timeframe."

Click-to-action is one of the most important recent issues in Internet advertising. It addresses the obsession some companies have with "last-click attribution." As stated earlier, last-click attribution is not necessarily a good benchmark for advertising effectiveness. The customer we described earlier who considered a St. Lucia vacation may have been very positively influenced by the content-based track created at the beginning "demand creation" phase of the buying cycle. When that customer clicked on the banner or search keyword that led to actually booking plane tickets, it was technically the "last click." But it wasn't the most important click.

The time between "click" and "action" depends a lot on the customer, the product, or the service. Travel, for example, can be urgent in some cases, and deliberate in others. A new laptop may have a long "click to action" time frame as the customer researches the products, compares prices and then buys. Content-based advertising is most often an early cycle strategy. By calling out the click to action time for pixel placement, advertisers can control how long they want to track the "click" and the "action" of content-based campaign. Defining the amount of time between click and action is a huge and underrated metric that helps advertisers know how their product or service should be advertised, and how long it should be advertised.

The click-to-action metric has ramification for publishers as well as advertisers. The Atlas Institute issued a report at the beginning of 2009 that introduces the related concept of "engagement mapping" or "eMap." An eMap report reveals how much engagement a web site delivers to the advertiser's customers. It calculates alternative ROI metrics, and scores each site on variables like reach, frequency, recency, ad format and ad size. The Atlas Institute believes that this may help justify budgets for media buys that appear to be underperforming through the "last-click attribution" lens. eMap insights will also define the key drivers of success for the advertiser and how inventory can be packaged and optimized to better attain key goals.

For advertisers, the Atlas Institute report states that "our research shows that vertical content buys have a greater role to play in today's media plans. Advertisers with a highly considered purchase or a long sales cycle will experience particularly pernicious exposure to the last-ad bias. Identify which buys are cost-efficiently contributing to the upper part of your purchase funnel by using more sophisticated conversion reporting like Engagement Mapping. The Engagement Mapping Factors Report can be run on any campaign tracked by Atlas, and will provide a snapshot of which sites are delivering reach and engagement to your customers beyond the last ad."

Regardless of whether it is Google, ADSDAQ, or both, content-based advertising is bringing positive challenges to the accepted thinking around Internet advertising, and bringing new opportunities for optimization. How it works is just as important as whether it works. Advertisers are maximizing demand among a group that's much more important than any bragging rights could ever be: Customers.

Three Keys to ADSDAQ Optimization:

1. Set performance goals: ADSDAQ automatically excludes underperforming web pages and adds impressions to high-performance pages. Focus on bid price and CTR as key performance goals.

2. Optimize: Bid price, CTR, and tracking pixels can all be adjusted as campaigns roll out.

3. Set click-to-action: ADSDAQ allows advertisers to address one of the cutting edge issues in Internet advertising. Setting click-to-action thresholds is a huge advantage of ASDSDAQ's optimization tools.

Customers Now

In the end, the success of a business depends on customers. Customers are the only real asset a business has. Products are just inventory unless someone buys them. If an ad campaign garners industry awards, internal praise and big buzz in the blogosphere, it means nothing if that ad campaign lacks the customer connection. As customer strategy author and pioneer Martha Rogers says: "Without customers you don't have a business, you have a hobby."

So it is with Internet advertising. Too often companies use Internet advertising because it's "hot" or because they don't want to position themselves behind the beat. No one wants to lack innovation in marketing. It just isn't cool. The coolest and most overlooked thing about Internet marketing is its laser connection to customers. It started that way in the late 90s when banners crowded most every ad page available. It continued to be about customers when new technologies made email the ubiquitous form of customer communication. It caught fire when Google redefined the entire concept of search. At its basic level, Google refocused search results on connecting to the customer, not pleasing the advertiser.

Now we enter the era of content-based advertising. It's still about customers. This book has made the case for considering content-based advertising as an essential part of the marketing arsenal. Email is essential for product information and customer engagement. Banners and other graphic executions make the Internet a branding vehicle, important to any customer image identification. Now they too are part of the content-based paradigm. Graphical ads have been previously limited to big brand advertisers because of the way they are typically bought. Now anyone can use a self-service application like Google AdWords or ContextWeb's ADSDAQ Exchange Buying Desk to place a graphical ad.

What is now available is a more complete approach – a whole new frontier of Internet marketing. Companies need to use the Internet for demand creation, customer acquisition and building contextual value. Content-based advertising is ready to be placed in the same "must-do" media strategy list as email, search, and graphic placements. This is a new way to approach Internet marketing. For the short term, companies like Google and ContextWeb and its ADSDAQ Exchange will play the biggest roles, but also expect more companies to embrace this new dynamic. As more advertisers look toward content-based advertising, more search engines and media companies will come out to meet them. Content-based advertising is *not* search engine advertising. There's very little search involved. You want to find new customers. Content-based advertising, by focusing first on content categories and then on actual content pages, takes the search out. You already found customers because you already found the content.

Content-based advertising is a tool that enables one more level of control over the campaign. It provides one more way for a company to compete for customers regardless of size or budget. It takes the promise of the Internet of the late 90s and moves it into a new decade. That promise was a connection to customers, and an ability to find new ones. Don't wait to follow this trend. Your customers are out there – now.

Enjoy David Szetela and *Customers Now* at your next event!

Enjoy David Szetela and Customers Now at your next event, show or conference. David Szetela is available for keynote presentations, panels and longer seminars and we can arrange for bulk purchasing and promotions with the Customers Now book.

Please contact us via www.CustomersNowBook.com for more information about speaking opportunities, bulk purchasing and promotions.

NOTES

NOTES

NOTES

NOTES

NOTES